Clement Mansfield Ingleby

Reflections Historical and Critical on the Revival of

Philosophy at Cambridge

Clement Mansfield Ingleby

Reflections Historical and Critical on the Revival of Philosophy at Cambridge

ISBN/EAN: 9783337072087

Printed in Europe, USA, Canada, Australia, Japan

Cover: Foto ©ninafisch / pixelio.de

More available books at **www.hansebooks.com**

REFLECTIONS

HISTORICAL AND CRITICAL,

ON

THE REVIVAL OF PHILOSOPHY

AT CAMBRIDGE.

BY

C. M. INGLEBY, M.A., LL.D.,

FOREIGN SECRETARY TO THE ROYAL SOCIETY OF LITERATURE.

CAMBRIDGE:

J. HALL AND SON.

———

1870.

THIS LITTLE VOLUME

IS

𝔊𝔯𝔞𝔱𝔢𝔣𝔲𝔩𝔩𝔶 𝔍𝔫𝔰𝔠𝔯𝔦𝔟𝔢𝔡

TO

JAMES HUTCHISON STIRLING,

LL.D. & F.R.C.S., EDIN

AUTHOR OF " THE SECRET OF HEGEL," ETC.

———

In recognition of his helping hand
Outstretcht to guide and hearten him, whose way
Lies through the perplext paths of this drear wood,
The awful maze of metaphysic lore,
The nodding horrour of whose shady brows
Threats the forlorn and wandering passenger.

PREFACE.

In the last century a decent modicum of Philosophy, principally drawn from three sterling English writers, Locke, Butler, and Clarke, was required of candidates for academical honours at Cambridge. This modicum, once representing substantial knowledge, dwindled down to a mere form and pretence, which mocked and wearied questionist and examiner alike. Two plain courses of reform were open to the University authorities, *i.e.* the Senate, and its Caput : to revive the comatose reality, or simply to abolish the deadly-lively semblance. They elected the latter alternative. Philosophy, even in the last stage of collapse, and abandoned to the tender mercies of physicians, who were both ignorant and unfriendly, and who, like Timon's associates, *throve and gave her over*, seemed disposed to contest the Academical *grace*, and, if die she must, to die hard. Like the fever-stricken sailor, in the story, who remonstrating with the person commissioned to heave him over, inly muttered " Stop, I ain't dead yet," she would have been considered outrageously fastidious, had she been particular to half an hour. Her decease (from inanition) was formally certified in the books of the Senate, on March 20, 1827, by Messrs. Wood, French, Peacock, Gwatkin, Whewell, Graham, Chevallier, and King. The reign of Mathematics and Physics, divorced, however, from experiment, was now absolute.

But despite this formality Philosophy was not dead ! The authors of *The Student's Guide* assure us that the new Tripos for the encouragement of Philosophy " was not the introduction of a new thing at Cambridge, but merely the revival and reformation of what under one form or other [*i.e.* another] had always existed there : " " all which I most powerfully and potently believe." Stricken down she was by a rigid catalepsy which simulated death *to the life.* But the antiquated Cambridge *clairvoyante* was *not* dead. Her unmanifested vitality was *recognised,* not by the University, but within the precincts of certain Colleges ; where Butler, Paley, Stewart, Cudworth, and Price, and in later times Whewell, formed the material of what was still done under the names of Metaphysics and Ethics. Jammed in and *foulée* between the dominant monopolies of Mathematics and Theology, **the** former of which assumed her very name (with an ironical prefix), and the latter not a few of her functions, she could scarcely draw her breath.

This monstrous state of things was maintained with complacency in the face of the great German movement, whose authors first laid firm and sure for aye the foundations of mental and moral science.

* * * * * * * *

In 1851 the Moral Sciences Tripos was established. *Nunc demum redit animus.* After nineteen years of the new *régime* it is time to take our bearings. Where are we, and whither are we sailing? Whither are we *bound?* is the more important inquiry. ·Perhaps our course is a great circle, to find ourselves at length *in statu quo anno* 1851, which would be a deplorable consummation for all concerned.

To reply to these questions is the object of the following pages. My work will be threefold; historical, critical, and didactic. My purpose is to trace the rise of the new *régime*; to examine into its working and results; and to make suggestions for its material improvement. It is further my intention to supplement the first and practical part of my work, by a theoretical discussion of the more impor-

tant topics embraced by the Moral Sciences Tripos.
Primarily, then, I address myself to the Board of
Moral Sciences Studies, and to the Examiners in
that Tripos; secondarily, to students of the Uni-
versity who are reading for the Moral Sciences
Honours.

CHAPTER I.

THE MONOPOLY OF MATHEMATICS.

IN every University, and in every College, there is a constant tendency towards the monopoly of some special department of education. At Oxford the monopoly has long been Classics; at Cambridge, Mathematics; at Edinburgh, Metaphysics, Logic, and Ethics. But the good sense of the academical authorities has, from time to time, applied some corrective or counterpoise to the exclusive cultivation of one kind of study, though such reforms have generally fallen short of the end contemplated, and, in some instances, have proved miserable failures.

The establishment of the Classical Tripos in 1824 was a laudable and successful attempt to restore the balance between Mathematics and Classics at Cambridge, but it was not till 1857 that it was placed on the same footing as the Mathematical Tripos. But this reform had but little, if any effect, on the degree or extent to which Philosophy was cultivated in the University. At no time in this century was Philosophy in any of its branches a prominent study at Cambridge. To be sure, a partial and inadequate encouragement was given it at some of the Colleges; but up to very recent times Locke's *Essay concerning Human Understanding*, and Paley's *Moral and Political*

Philosophy were the only philosophical books that entered into the University Course ; and an acquaintance with these was required for the Common Degree only. Logic was not taught at all, and Ethics (save in the perverted sense of Paley) was equally neglected.

We may safely say, then, that in 1833, when Professor Sedgwick put forth his able *Discourse on the Studies of the University*, Philosophy (save what little might be gleaned from Locke) was at a discount at Cambridge. Unfortunately Professor Sedgwick's work did not mend matters there. Half a loaf is better than no bread ; and though Locke's *Essay* is beyond controversy at once the most unreadable and the most vacillating treatise ever printed in England on the Philosophy of Mind, yet there is good work to be done upon it, and a vigorous intellect might make it the platform of a true system. Even at this day an expurgated *Locke*, with a condensed running commentary from the hand of a Kantian, would be a valuable text-book. It was not that Professor Sedgwick argued the metaphysical question amiss, or that, having argued it well, he lacked influence to bring his argument to bear, and to translate theory into practice. He had both the rights of it, and the influence in the counsels of the Caput. It was, by no means, difficult to prove that the study of Locke, *et præterea nihil*, was useless, and even damaging, to the education of the student. Professor Sedgwick did this, and more. But his work was almost wholly negative ; and his influence was wholly so. In short, he, and the authorities who agreed with him, swept Locke away, but put nothing in his place ! Paley still dragged on a sickly and waning existence in the curriculum for the " Poll " ; so that we may say that, from the epoch of Locke's banishment, the University required of its students no Metaphysics or Logic of any kind, and no Ethics of the right kind. Philosophy was thenceforth a dead letter ; though it had, here and there, a bare *collegiate* recognition, it had no *locus standi* in the University. Such was the true state of the case when Sir William Hamilton, of Edinburgh, came to the rescue. The " desperate hook " of Richard Bentley seemed to have been appropriated by the Northern Professor ; *slashing* would have described him as accurately as it did Bentley. Learned beyond all his contemporaries, boorishly ignorant of Mathematics, he conceived a hatred of mathematicians worthy of Goethe. All he wanted was a decent excuse for taking the field ; and the coveted opportunity was soon furnished by the publication, in 1835, of the late Professor Whewell's pamphlet, entitled *Thoughts on the Study of Mathematics as a Part of a Liberal Education*. Eagerly did Sir William seize the occasion ; and forthwith appeared, what had been, doubtless, long prepared *nunc pro tunc*, his famous article on the study of Mathematics, in the *Edinburgh Review* (January, 1836). He here asserted that the University of Cambridge, by their partial, not to say exclusive, encouragement of mathematical and physical pursuits, had "exactly reversed

every principle of academical policy." Five grounds
are specified. He then proceeds to suggest reform.
"With all its defects, there is, even now, in the spirit
of the place, what, were its mighty means all as well
directed as some already are, would raise it in every
faculty, in every department, to the highest rank
among the European Universities. Some parts of
the reform are difficult, and must be accomplished
from without. Others are comparatively easy, and,
it is not too much to hope, may be determined from
within. Of these, the first and most manifest improvement would be the establishment of *three Triposes of co-ordinate and independent honours ;* of which
one should comprise the different departments of
philosophy proper, ancient and modern." This was
the suggestion; but it was not realised till nearly
sixteen years afterwards.

In reply to this article, which Mr. De Morgan
calls "a curious and powerful exhibition of weak-
ness," Professor Whewell contributed a letter to the
Edinburgh Review (April, 1836), which he republished
at the end of his work *On the Principles of English
University Education*, 1837. He had, in his pamphlet,
incautiously made the statement that Mathematics is
a better means of forming logical habits than Logic
itself; on this issue Sir William Hamilton thought
to snatch an easy victory, by demonstrating that
Mathematics was but an applied logic, Logic applied
to necessary matter ; and forasmuch as Logic might
be applied to contingent matter, resulting in philosophical science and common reasoning, it is plain

that Mathematics is but one of two applied logics, and is the one which educates the fewer faculties. He therefore contended that there is no more contrast between Mathematics and Logic, as instruments of education, than between a part and a whole.

In his haste to convict his opponent of an oversight, Hamilton strangely overlooked one of the most obvious distinctions in the world. He points out, indeed, that Logic applied to contingent matter is just as much Logic, as Logic applied to necessary matter; but for once he failed to discriminate between the necessity of the illative process, and the necessity of the premises. Logic, as logic, is a necessary science. Its study has as little to do with the truth or falsehood of any proposition that is not a truism, as with the psychological laws on which it rests. Accordingly, when Dr. Whewell says that its operation is best illustrated by geometrical deductions, it is no answer to say that the logic of Geometry does not educate the Intuitive Intellect, the faculty which furnishes premises for reasoning, and laws of psychology; for *no logic can do that*. A logical induction is just as necessary a piece of reasoning as a logical deduction; and there is as entire an acceptance of the premises in the one as in the other. Hamilton's answer, then, was, so far, no answer at all. It was not enough for him to aver, that the logic of Mathematics was a partial and inadequate instrument of educating the Reason, for *all logic is that;* but he was bound to have gone further, and shown that logical habits of mind are better acquired from the study of theoretical logic,

than from the study of one of two applied logics—
Mathematics; or to allow his opponent, on the issue
of Logic *v*. Mathematics, to take the palm *pro con-
fesso*. He did neither; but gave his powerful and
well-stored mind to the task of proving (what had
not been expressly denied) that the study of Mathematics is not, what Philosophy is, a means of educating the perceptive faculty. Judgment on the former
issue must have gone against him by default, but
for an oversight of his opponent. Dr. Whewell, not
satisfied with a good position, had gone a step too
far; he had asserted that Geometry presented the
student with " the most natural fallacies," on which
account its study was a good logical exercise. Now
the " fantastic tricks" of words, the *idola fori*, are the
chief bane of general reasoning. "For one instance of
logomachy," writes Coleridge, " I have met with ten
instances of *logodædaly*, or verbal legerdemain." This
besetting vice infects everything but Mathematics.
There it cannot intrude; for the language of Mathematics being exact and precise, and having no
" second intention," is strictly convertible with
thought. Accordingly all sophistry is, by the nature
of the case, driven out of the terms into the forms
of reasoning, and there it is necessarily detected.
Hence it is plain that the most accomplished and
advanced student of Geometry is as little upon his
guard against, as little able to detect, the chief fallacies of ordinary reasoning, as before he had read
a page of Euclid. For such an end, a thorough
analysis of the more famous sophisms of the Ancients

would be of more service than a knowledge of all the Geometry in the world. Mercilessly did Sir William Hamilton expose Dr. Whewell's mistake; yet, strange to say, Dr. Whewell repeats it in his tract *Of a Liberal Education in General* with as innocent a confidence in its correctness as if Sir William Hamilton had not utterly refuted it ten years before.

But if Whewell is thus at variance with Hamilton on the question of Geometrical Mathematics, he is entirely with him on that of Analytical Mathematics. Where Hamilton's argument is absolutely conclusive, there Whewell affects to ignore him : but where Hamilton writes without either knowledge or reason, there Whewell, equally slighting him, is so enamoured of his cause, that he wrests the weapons from the hands of his opponent, and does battle *on the same side*. (*Of a Liberal Education in General*, pp. 40 and 41, 1845.) This is no mere metaphor. For instance : Whewell coolly appropriates Hamilton's imagery of railroad travelling, to express the utter inutility of the analytical method in Mathematics, either as a *gymnastic* or as a *cathartic* of the student's intellect. " If," says he, " the attempt be made to so employ it, it will not only be worthless, but highly prejudicial to men's minds." (Ibid. p. 55.) By this the late Master of Trinity apparently meant to assert that Analytical Mathematics cannot do the work with which he credits Geometrical Mathematics : viz. the education of the Discursive Intellect. But is this a valid objection to making the study of Algebra a principal means to a liberal education ? Is it not as plain as a pikestaff that Discourse is but a crutch for Intuition ? To a really strong intellect, a proposition of Euclid, the demonstration of which is made to depend on a long and tedious series of axioms and theorems, may be quite as self-evident as an axiom. There are many men to whom the 47th is instantly seen to be true by the aid of a special diagram, without the knowledge of a single foregoing proposition. To such a mind the practice of ratiocination is not only superfluous but injurious —just as injurious as the use of crutches would be to a man who had the use of his limbs. The Reason in its higher functions is, at least, *not strengthened* by this wearisome routine of discursive reasoning. So, then, it is no objection to Analytical Mathematics, that they do not do this work. Now the theorems of Algebra are, for the most part, *immediate* inferences from intuitional *data*, as Dr. Whewell virtually allows. He says, indeed, that every step in an Algebraical demonstration *may be* viewed as a syllogism, of which the major is, "Things that are equal to the same thing are equal to one another ;" and the minor, the statement that two quantities or expressions are equal to a third. That is correct. But it would be a most unnatural and preposterous mode of analysing the reasoning of an algebraical demonstration ; for in such a syllogism the only reasoning material to the science would be shut up in *one* of the premises ! It would be just as rational to say, that all *mediate* reasoning proceeds by a syllogism of which the major is Aristotle's *dictum de omni et nullo ;* and the minor, a statement of two premises conformably to the *dictum.*

The only correct analysis of the mediate reasoning of Algebra is one which assumes the *Transitive Principle :* viz. If A is B, and B is C, C is D ; first enunciated by Mr. De Morgan. (*Syllabus of a Proposed System of Logic,* 1860, p. 47.) Interesting as such analysis is, it is of less importance than the intuitive principles according to which the *immediate* inferences of Algebra proceed. It is just because the algebraist does not bring into prominence the *discursive* operations of his mind that the study of Algebra is so important; for it thereby stimulates the energy of the Intuition to discover the principles of immediate inference. The more productive is the Intellect of the student, the less does he require demonstration ; and conversely, the less he finds himself dependent upon demonstration, the greater assurance he has that his Intellect is undergoing progressive improvement. It is, then, no inherent quality of Geometry which unfits that science for serving as a first-rate intellectual gymnastic; it is the accident of the method by which it is taught ; and accordingly Analytical Geometry is, in some respects, a better athletic of the Reason than Pure Analysis.

The danger attending the study of Analytical Mathematics consists in the constant temptation held out to the student (who has, of course, to learn its formulæ by rote) to believe that an equation is true, without perceiving the reason of its truth, simply because, as a rule of art, it is found to yield true results in

c

practice: and this danger is fully set forth both by Sir
William S. Hamilton, of Edinburgh, in the article
already described, and by Sir William R. Hamilton, of
Dublin, in his admirable treatise on *Conjugate Functions*.
(*Transactions of the Royal Irish Academy*, vol. xvii.)*
But the Scotch Hamilton was not satisfied with
the attempt to disprove the utility of Mathematics as

---

* "The study of Algebra may be pursued in three very
different schools, the Practical, the Philological, or the Theoretical, according as ease of operation, or symmetry of expression, or clearness of thought (the *agere*, the *fari*, or the *sapere*),
is eminently prized and sought for. The Practical person
seeks a Rule which he may apply, the Philological person seeks
a Formula which he may write, the Theoretical person
seeks a Theorem on which he may meditate. The felt imper-
fections of Algebra are of three answering kinds. The
Practical Algebraist complains of imperfection when he finds
his Instrument limited in power; when a rule, which he could
happily apply to many cases, can be hardly or not at all
applied by him to some new case; when it fails to enable him
to do or to discover something else, in some other Art or
in some other Science, to which Algebra with him was
but subordinate, and for the sake of which and not for its own
sake, he studied Algebra. The Philological Algebraist complains of imperfection, when his language presents him with
an Anomaly; when he finds an exception disturb the simplicity
of his Notation, or the symmetrical structure of his Syntax;
when a Formula must be written with precaution, and a Sym-
bolism is not universal. The Theoretical Algebraist complains of imperfection, when the clearness of his Contemplation
is obscured; when the Reasonings of his Science seem anywhere to oppose each other, or become in any part too
complex or too little valid for his belief to rest firmly upon
them; or when, though trial may have taught him that
a rule is useful, or that a formula gives the results, he cannot
prove that rule, nor understand that formula: when he
cannot rise to intuition from induction, or cannot look beyond
the signs to the things signified."—pp. 293-4.

an instrument of education ; but he set up Philosophy as the study which could securely effect the very
results ignored by Mathematics, and on this ground
denounced its neglect at Cambridge. Now every
man of common sense, who has had the slightest experience of tuition, knows that it is not enough to state,
or even to prove, that a particular subject of reasoning
is, by its very nature, a first-rate gymnastic of the
Intellect. To recommend a study, with no further
assistance, is like the excellent advice sometimes given
by the medical practitioner to his indigent patient, *to
live generously and drink plenty of old port wine.* Dr.
Whewell, in his letter to the *Edinburgh Review,* allowing *pro certo* the Reviewer's plea on behalf of Mental
Science, and actually then having in mind the practi-
cability of establishing a Philosophy Tripos at Cambridge, asked him to specify the work or works in
which Philosophy might be taught with the same
security, or promise of success, as Mathematics are
taught at Cambridge by the aid of certain well-known
works of credit. Hamilton *in effect,* speaking meta-
phorically, recommended Whewell to leave off dram-
drinking, and for the future to drink only the Elixir
of Life. "But where, in the name of common sense,
can I procure this Elixir ?" demands the sensible Mathematician of the Common Sense Philosopher. For
myself, I can never read Hamilton's reply without
laughing. He shuffles and evades the question : the
demand, he says, is ill-timed, is founded on a mistake as to the issue raised, &c. &c. The Elixir of Life
is to Hamilton a nectar which flows not exclusively

from this or that spring, like your Mathematics, but trickles in countless rills, in various volumes, and in various degrees of purity. Dr. Whewell, in fact, had no business to ask so impertinent a question. Impertinent it would doubtless have been, if premature : but, if premature, so also was the suggestion, which Hamilton himself had made, for the establishment of a Philosophy Tripos. No one felt greater assurance than Hamilton himself that none of those rills could be depended on for yielding the liquor free from foreign admixture ; nor did he believe that the great toxicologist had yet arisen who possessed the secret of eliminating or neutralising the pernicious ingredients. On the whole one may be pretty sure, that the drink, which might in irony be called Hamilton's *Entire*, was the particular elixir which the great Celt had in view, with which we are at length made thoroughly familiar, and which in its turn has been tested by Mill, Stirling, Boulton, and many others, and which has been found utterly worthless. This, however, he would certainly have recommended, but for the untoward fact that he had never succeeded in prevailing on himself to go through the necessary drudgery of composition (not to insist on the severe toil of redintegration, if that were possible), and so to commit himself to a complete system of Philosophy. His notes on Reid were then and still remain fragmentary; his Lectures were then only in manuscript ; and his Philosophical contributions to the *Edinburgh Review* were upon special and subordinate topics, not then, nor since, gathered up into one concatenated scheme. Evasion, then, instead of recommendation, was all Dr. Whewell got by his inquiry. Thenceforth, like a wise man, as he was, he eschewed discussion with one whose sole strength seemed to lie in profitless controversy. He returned to the subject in various works,* but with the exception of a passing allusion in his *Principles of University Education*, he eschewed the man in dealing with the subject. On other subjects, however, Dr. Whewell did not disdain to give Hamilton's views systematic

---

* These are—
Principles of University Education, 1837.
Of a Liberal Education in General, 1845.
The Philosophy of the Inductive Sciences: Book XIII. Chapter III. The first of these contains the reprint of
I. Whewell's Letter to the Edinburgh Reviewer. Besides this, Hamilton's Review received other replies.
II. The Study of Mathematics, as conducive to the Development of the Intellectual Powers. By Professor Chevallier, of Durham.
III. A section of Mr. Devy's Logic. (Bohn, 1854, p. 374.)
IV. Fragmentary remarks in Mr. De Morgan's Formal Logic (1847), and in his papers contributed to the *Transactions of the Cambridge Philosophical Society*; especially that On the Syllogism, No. V.; his Notes in *Notes and Queries* (2nd Series, Vol. VI. pp. 125, 209 and 292); his Syllabus of a Proposed System of Logic (1860, pp. 43-44); a Review of Hamilton's *Lectures* in the *Athenæum* (Nov. 10 and 24, 1860), acknowledged by Mr. De Morgan; and some other communications to that periodical.
V. A correction of Hamilton's assertion respecting the τὸ ὅτι and τὸ διότι of Aristotle, in the late Professor Boole's Mathematical Analysis of Logic, 1847.

refutation : as in the *History of Scientific Ideas* and the *Philosophy of Discovery.* In the former work (vol. ii. p. 37, book vi. chap. iii. note) he likens Hamilton's "barren ontological distinctions" to " the speculations of the eminent schoolmen of the most sterile periods of the dark ages "; and the substance of this censure takes a still more depreciatory form in Chapter xxvi. of the *Philosophy of Discovery.*

CHAPTER II.

THE RECOGNITION OF MENTAL AND MORAL SCIENCE.

THE famous Edinburgh polemic, against the Study
of Mathematics as a means of mental culture, pro-
voked, as we have seen, the self-complacent, not
to say contemptuous, criticism of the late Master
of Trinity : yet, curious to relate, it was by Dr.
Whewell's influence that the practical suggestion of
Hamilton was at length adopted and realised. In
1851 the Moral Sciences Tripos was instituted, and
as a special encouragement to the cultivation of
Moral Philosophy, Dr. Whewell offered three prizes,
two of £15 each, and one of £20, to be awarded
in every year of his Professorship to those questionists who should exhibit the greatest proficiency
in that subject; the two former to Commencing
Bachelors, the latter to Middle Bachelors—a distinction which prevailed in the Class Lists of that
Tripos till the remarkable epoch of 1860.

In 1855 our late lamented Master resigned his
Professorship, and was succeeded therein by the late
Rev. John Grote; and on the death of that excel-
lent scholar and worthy man in 1866, the present
Professor, the Rev. Frederick Denison Maurice,
M.A., of Exeter College, Oxford, was elected to that
Chair. The appointment of a distinguished philo-

sopher and divine of the sister-University to a Cambridge Professorship, was calculated to provoke the most opposite feelings. To import a stranger into a University office has the air of a very humiliating confession. Given that Cambridge, among all her graduates, did not possess the right man for the place, or possessing, could not discover him, or having discovered, did not promote him, such an appointment must, *on its own merits*, have given the liveliest satisfaction to all concerned. *First*, it was a direct acknowledgment of that catholicity and community which ought ever to unite the two leading Universities, who are at once coadjutors and corrivals in the great work of raising and strengthening the English mind and character; and also, indirectly, a repudiation (I do not say renunciation) of that exclusiveness which is so common and so pardonable in the great centres of education. *Secondly*, it reciprocated the policy of the sister-University, in choosing (in the preceding year) a Cambridge man, Professor Clifton, to fill the Chair of Experimental Philosophy at Oxford. *Thirdly*, it conferred at once a high honour and an important trust upon a divine who, for upholding a perfectly legitimate doctrinal distinction, had been treated with monstrous injustice and shameful indignity "in another place"; and who had subsequently drawn the sword with such telling effect in defence of the very basis of our Religious Philosophy, *and therefore of our Religion*, against the shallow and pretentious dialectics of the Bampton Lecturer of 1858.

But, alas! these several grounds of satisfaction rested on the assumption that Philosophy was at a discount on the banks of the Cam. If Cambridge had a sufficiently good man for the place, the appointment of a stranger was surely inexpedient: if Cambridge had not a sufficiently good man for the place, her insolvency was deplorable, though the appointment of a stranger was inevitable. Satisfaction, then, resting on dissatisfaction is the only " frame of mind" into which this appointment can be received. At best, we can only say, we rejoice in Mr. Maurice's success, because had Cambridge not gone so far she would have fared worse!

The University of Cambridge, then, possesses an efficient lecturer on Mental and Moral Science, and a Tripos for testing the merits of those who have profited by his lectures. What else? Why, I am sorry to say, not much. At the present time there are but two prizes at Cambridge for the direct encouragement of philosophical studies; viz. the Burney Prize and the Hare Prize. Of these the latter *cannot be* awarded for an exercise on any philosophical subject save " the History of Greek or Roman Philosophy"; and the former *may be* awarded to an exercise in Divinity. However, the examiners have shown a wise disposition to make these, and even the Hulsean Prize, rewards for excellence in philosophical subjects.

Of prizes for the encouragement of logical studies —there are none. This paragraph is so far like the chapter on snakes in Horrebow's *Natural History (Norway)*, or that in Pontoppidan's *Iceland*.

The Moral Sciences Tripos now embraces four great subjects—*Moral Philosophy, Mental Philosophy, Logic,* and *Political Economy.* At first, and for five years after, an exactitude was attempted in the classification of questionists, which has since been abandoned. The intrusion of Modern History, Jurisprudence, and English Law into this Tripos (by the side of Moral Philosophy) perhaps rendered it expedient to prefix (as was done) numbers to the names of the questionists, referring to footnotes which indicated who were distinguished in each branch. The expediency was based on an inexpediency: for three of the four subjects had no business there at all. When the Tripos was reconstituted in 1856, and Moral Philosophy, Mental Philosophy, Logic, and Political Economy became the co-ordinate subjects of the Tripos, the refinement which had been previously attempted was wisely discontinued. In fact, the practice, which was always objectionable as burdening the Class Lists with an abortive running commentary, must have become more and more intolerable as the lists grew bigger. However, the equally absurd practice of furnishing separate Lists of Middle Bachelors and Commencing Bachelors was adopted in 1852, and continued down to 1860, when a merciful providence intervened. Not a single candidate of either status presented himself in that year! So the baffled examiners were unable, *ex necessitate,* to continue the prescribed division, simply because they had nothing to divide. In that memorable year none was distinguished, not even by his absence, for none was present. Had but one well-prepared questionist presented himself, though unfortunately he could not be both a Middle and a Commencing Bachelor at once, he would have enjoyed the rare distinction of a class to himself, unmolested by invidious or contumelious criticism.

The disconcerted authorities then changed their tactics. Having found by experience that *one* Tripos Examination in the year was too much, they forthwith established *two;* one in February, and one in November! The new plan, however, disappointed their expectations, and it was abandoned in 1862; from which time the authorities, made wise by experience, have uniformly done what they should have done from the first, viz. held one examination in each year, the questionists who pass it being arranged in three classes. There they stand without note or comment, until in after years they distinguish themselves in public life; education, literature, science, or art.

After various reverses, then, the Tripos, if not a great, is an accomplished fact. It has held on its way, with variable fortunes, into its twentieth year. During that period 159 students have obtained its honours in nineteen examinations; that is to say, 82 in the First Class (the names of two occurring twice, *i.e.* as Commencing Bachelors and as Middle Bachelors), 45 in the Second Class (the name of one occurring twice), and 32 in the Third Class.

We may say that a decided success has been achieved; but it is nevertheless true that the Moral

Sciences Tripos has not yet taken the rank it deserves, and which, I feel sure, it is destined to take. At present it has to contend with three classes in the University ; those who do not believe in the possibility of Metaphysical Science, are therefore opposed to any provision for its culture : those who are quite indifferent to its pretensions and its demands : and those who take up with a sort of philosophical syncretism, founded for the most part on physiology. I am not sure whether the first or the third is the class most detrimental to the success of Philosophy . at Cambridge. The majority of the leading mathematicians of the United Kingdom belong to one or other of these classes. If I may judge from those of my own personal acquaintance, (and they include many of the oldest and the most famous,) I should say that the majority do not believe in Metaphysics at all : and yet even some of these are solicitous to promote the culture of Logic, and are not averse to a temperate dose of philosophical literature, as a factor in liberal education : the rest of that majority rejoice in the breach that is believed to exist between the mathematician and the metaphysician, and are not backward to widen it. As an instance of what I mean, I may refer to a discussion which followed the reading of a paper written by Mr. W. R. Smith, at a meeting of the Royal Society of Edinburgh, towards the close of 1868, in which the attack and defence were equally deplorable. I am not aware whether the Cambridge Philosophical Society is ever discredited by such a display of acrimony and unfairness as was " aired " on that occasion. I should think not: and yet I am confident that the materials for it are not far to seek.

Be that as it may, of this we may be sure, that so long as Mathematics and Classics are the *beaten tracks* to the goal of a College Fellowship, and Metaphysics is but a *squirrel run*, by following out which the student will find himself " up a tree," whence he can command a wide range of speculation, but is none the nearer to the modest object of his wishes : few undergraduates will care to purchase their philosophy at so great a personal sacrifice.

Let us apply to this question a simple test. What College Fellowships are or have been held by those whose names are in the Moral Sciences Tripos?

The following table will answer this inquiry in full :—

Name of Fellow.	His College.	His place in Math. Tri.	Ditto in Clas. Tri.	Ditto in Mo. Sc.T.	Year of last.
Hort	Trinity . .	53 Jun. Op.	α , 5	I , 4	1851
Gorham . . .	,, . .	14 Wr.	β , 4	I , 2	1852
Simmonds . . .	Jesus . .	28 Wr.	. . .	I , 3	,,
Mayor	St. John's .	. . . .	α , 2	II , 2	,,
Perceval . . .	Trinity Hall	. . . .	. . .	II , 1 & 2	1852 & 3
Ellis . . .	Trinity . .	9 Jun. Op.	α , 9	I , 2	1853
Seeley	,, . .	6 Wr.	α , 16	I , 3	,,
Shield	Jesus . .	. . . .	α , 13	II , 1	1855
Droop	Trinity . .	3 Wr.	. . .	I , 1	,,
Webster . . .	,, . .	14 Jun. Op.	α , 5	I , 4	1856
Manley	Clare . .	21 Wr. ·	. . .	I , 1	1858
Cobb	Trinity . .	. . . .	α , 11	I , 1	1861
Pearson . . .	St. John's .	. . . .	. . .	I , 1	1863
Myers . . .	Trinity . .	. . . .	α , 3	I , 2	1864
Taylor	Clare . .	. . . .	. . .	I , 1	1865
Mansel	Trinity . .	. . . .	α , 6	I , 2	1866
Maccoll	Downing .	. . . .	β , 5	I , 4	,,
Cox	St. John's .	. . . .	α , 6	I , 3	1867
Gwatkin . . .	,, . .	36 Wr.	α , 10	I , 4	,,
Verdon	,, . .	8 Wr.	β , 19	I , 1	1868

The First Classes in the Moral Sciences Tripos
give us, as I have said, eighty-two names. Of
these, twenty are late or present Fellows of Colleges. But, as appears by the foregoing table,
two of these twenty gentlemen were double-first-
classmen, in Mathematics and in Classics; and, in
the whole, there are seven Wranglers, and eleven first-
classmen, Classics; so that there are exactly sixteen,
of whom we may safely assert that their Mathematics
or their Classics, or both, was the favouring gale
which wafted them into the comfortable haven of a
College Fellowship. I am not here denying that
a certain amount of philosophical power is implied
in a high mathematical degree, nor that a certain
amount of philosophical erudition is implied in a
high classical degree. Grant that it is so; and consequently that, though the Moral Sciences degree was
not the cause of their College Fellowships, it may
have been to some extent a consequence of their
mathematical or classical excellence. But the table
authorises no presumption whatever that the Moral
Sciences degree was the moving consideration to the
Fellowship, unless, perhaps, in the cases of two
gentlemen, of St. John's and Clare respectively, who
did not take the usual Honours. The reasonable inference is that, of these twenty, sixteen obtained their
Fellowships for Mathematics or for Classics, or for
both; that one obtained his Fellowship for Civil Law;
and that two, at most, obtained theirs for their philosophical attainments. Two out of eighty-two first-
classmen in the Moral Sciences Tripos have found,

let us hope, that Tripos to be a by-way to pro-
motion! It is just so that the *philosophia prima* is
recognised by the Colleges of this University.

In point of fact, of so little worldly advantage is it
to a student to be distinguished in the new Tripos
that sometimes, even with the concurrence of mathematical or classical proficiency, he cannot obtain a
College Fellowship. Messrs. Sharpe, Lloyd, Mounsey,
Gedge, and others, were first-classmen in the Moral
Sciences, and each was a Wrangler or a first-class-
man in Classics; but their names are not found
among the late or present Fellows of Colleges. In
the case of some of these gentlemen, there may have
been other reasons for this want of success; yet the
cumulative evidence convinces me that their devotion
to Philosophy was bought very dear. It has long
been thought *shady* to go out in Law : it is, I fear,
thought still *shadier* to go out in Morals; for the
highway to preferment is evidently quite other than
that. At Cambridge, Moral Philosophy, like virtue,
is its own reward. It is in vain to look for either
thoroughly efficient teaching and training, or large
class-lists in the Moral Sciences Tripos till this state
of things is at an end. It is on the Colleges, rather
than the University, that the chief blame should be
cast; as theirs is the duty and the power of efficient
reform. Unfortunately the chance is small of co-
operation among them, with this or any other object, as
is shown by their answers to the Syndicate appointed
to consider the means of establishing a *working*
Professorship of Experimental Physics, the existing

Professorship being that *merely in name.* The Colleges will do little or nothing for Natural Science; and we may be sure they will do nothing for Philosophy. Meanwhile let us bear in mind that the wealth of the University is locked up in the Colleges; and it is intolerable that the Master, Seniors and Fellows of a College should constitute a close corporation, existing out of relation to the crying wants of the University. The editor of *Nature* (April 7, 1870) well remarks on the recent obstructiveness of the Colleges in the matter of Experimental Physics,—" It makes us seriously think whether the time has not come when the State should exercise more control over the enormous revenues of these old Colleges, which seem determined to go on in the old track." The time is *not* yet come : public opinion has not yet been brought to bear on the College authorities : but in the event of their proving inaccessible to that influence, as they seem to be at present to the demands of common sense, it may well happen that the Legislature will force upon them an administration of their vast resources according to the pressing wants of the Academical Community.

It is to be hoped, however, that the Senate will discharge its own simple duty, and establish a Professorship, co-ordinate with, or accessory to, the Knightbridge Professorship of Moral Philosophy, embracing the departments of Metaphysics and Logic.

The conduct of the Moral Sciences Tripos is committed by the Senate to a kind of Syndicate, called

" The Board of Moral Sciences Studies." Its business is to nominate Examiners, select books for study and examination, and generally to regulate the Tripos. Under the present system, four Examiners being actually appointed, two go out by rotation, and two fresh ones are nominated by the Board and elected by the Senate. The Board consists of the Regius Professor of Civil Law, the Professors of Moral Philosophy, Modern History, and Political Economy, the Examiners for the Moral Sciences Tripos in the current and preceding years, and three members of the Senate elected by Grace ; one of these three retires by rotation on November 20th in every year, and his place is supplied by election at the next ensuing Congregation. The Professor of Moral Philosophy is the chairman of the Board, or, if you will, the foreman of the jury.

We judge of the efficiency of this tribunal by its resolutions. These concern (1) the Examiners nominated by them ; (2) The List of Books approved by them ; (3) the Examination-papers to which they implicitly give their sanction. These three points I shall now consider *seriatim*.

CHAPTER III.

THE CHOICE OF EXAMINERS IN THE MORAL SCIENCES TRIPOS.

As a rule, the proclivities of an Examiner may be inferred from the character of his Examination-papers. Except in the case of elaborate dissimulation, a paper set by a mathematician would show traces of the mathematical mind, and one set by a classic would bear the impress of scholarly research. The fault of such papers would just consist in this, that the best logician, *as such*, or the best metaphysician, *as such*, would not be able to obtain the highest number of marks ; but, the papers being in effect framed with a mathematical or a classical bias, a second-rate logician or metaphysician, whose knowledge and power were supplemented by mathematics or classics, would be able to work the papers with a decided advantage over his betters.

In the Examination-papers in Moral Philosophy, of 1868, the following questions occur :—

" ' This objection hits the Cyrenaics sharply. It does not touch Epicurus.' Explain the difference between the Cyrenaics and Epicurus as to the nature of Pleasure."

"By what *argumentum ad hominem* does Cicero endeavour to confute the opinion of his friend Torquatus, that Pleasure and Pain are the ultimate objects of all pursuit? How does Torquatus answer the argument? Do you remember any passages from any modern authors which may illustrate the charge or the defence?"

The only exception that can be taken to them is one having reference to economy. The number of questions in this subject being limited to some twenty-five, or at most thirty, it stands to reason that there is but little margin for questions like these, which only touch the outskirts of the main topic, and are rather a test of classical *reading* than of philosophical *thought*. In one paper seven such questions occur in succession! Now the danger of entrusting the Examination to classical scholars, *as such*, is just that of overcharging the papers with questions of that kind, so as to crowd out the essentials of the subject. In the papers of 1868 we have the corresponding vice—*i.e.* the danger realised.

In the Examination-papers in Logic, of 1869, the following questions occur :—

"Explain to what extent a rigid and symbolical language, like that of Algebra, may be made useful, or is permissible, in scientific and philosophical investigation."

" 'To find the chance of the recurrence of an event already observed, divide the number of times the event has been observed, increased by one, by the same number increased by two.' What logical objections may be made to this rule of succession?"

In justice, let me say, that in those papers the

D 2

danger which these questions suggest is not realised, and the sample I have given, with two others, constitutes the whole stock of such questions. Nor can these two be objected to: nay, as to the latter, I rejoice to know that students are invited to the consideration of the eminently interesting branch of speculation to which it belongs. The sample, however, will fulfil the purpose of illustrating my meaning in asserting that the Examination-papers gain or lose efficiency according to the bent of the Examiner. Questions of either kind being allowed to overcharge the papers, the result must be adverse to the metaphysical expert, and the more adverse in proportion to the amount of his special qualifications; while the classic or the mathematician, with a smattering of philosophy, will easily win his way to a first class. The dangers I have indicated spring of course out of the selection of Examiners in the Moral Sciences who are not known to be proficient in the specialities of the Tripos. In all probability the Board of Moral Sciences Studies has never seriously considered the matter in this light. It is too much the habit with educated men to look upon philosophy as an old-fashioned or a new-fangled game, which may serve admirably as a *diversion* from the primary studies of the University, but cannot be allowed to compete with Mathematics and Classics, as if it were a self-supporting science. At most, it is regarded as a laudable πάρεργον or *by-work* for men whose best energies have been engrossed with the dead languages, or with Mathematics and Physics.

It is thought sufficient if the gentlemen nominated by the Board are distinguished for their classical learning and sound scholarship, or for their mathematical training ; especially so, if they are known to have *plowtered* in the shallows of philosophical literature, either as authors on their own account, or as contributors to the periodical press.

It is high time to awake out of that childish dream. It is not enough that the Examiner can construe with some precision and intelligence his Plato and his Aristotle, or that he can solve a differential equation and evaluate a definite integral. The expenditure of intellectual power, in the diligent prosecution of either of those two departments of knowledge which now constitute the great business of college life, is incompatible with high philosophical excellence, except in a few extraordinary cases, such as those of Leibnitz, Kant, Hegel, and perhaps Sir W. S. Hamilton. But, even in reference to these instances, somewhat may be said for a strict limitation of the field of study. Hamilton assuredly might have been a much greater abstract thinker, had his learning been less encyclopædic. Be that as it may, it is a matter of fact that neither the classical nor the mathematical expert does, as a rule, acquire philosophical power ; and consequently classical scholars, *as such*, and mathematicians, *as such*, are *primâ facie* disqualified for the office of Examiners in Philosophy. Besides this, there is a subordinate reason why the choice of the Board should not, as a rule, fall upon them, viz. the importance of inspiring the confidence of the world without both in the nominors and in the nominees. Incompetency or partiality might, on the strength of such nominations, be charged on the Board, *especially when the nomination falls on some of its own members ;* otherwise, it might be reasonably contended that the Moral Sciences Tripos is a mere adjunct to the Classical Tripos, answering to *science* in the *Literæ Humaniores* at Oxford.

The principle I am now contending for has been always observed in the Mathematical and Classical Triposes. In the former, with the view of ensuring an effective *personnel*, and also of inspiring confidence in its efficiency, it has from very early times been an inflexible rule with the authorities, that the Moderators and Examiners should be *selected* from those who have obtained *very high* places among the Wranglers. Generally the Moderator or Examiner is a senior, second, or third Wrangler. Two cases only have occurred of a *seventh* Wrangler being appointed to that office—viz. in 1839 and 1840-1, and one case only of an eighth Wrangler being appointed to it—viz. the eminent private tutor and author, Mr. Walton. The line is drawn there ; and it is most unlikely that his case will be made into a precedent. Custom founded on ancient precedent and sound reason disqualifies all below the seventh place from taking part in the examinations of the Mathematical Tripos. This custom is surely, on all accounts, most wise and salutary. It is the great security, as well of efficiency as of fairness. When has either of those indispensable qualities been called in question ? I never heard the faintest innuendo that,

in any examination, the papers had been faulty, or
the arrangement of the questionists unfair. The
utmost that has ever been said, in the way of adverse
criticism, is, that book-work (which any man of good
memory can cram) is usually too highly marked, and
that the divisions of the classes are sometimes arbi-
trary or partial. It is certain that book-work alone
can give a man a good place in the Wranglers. I
call to mind the case of Mr. W——, who obtained
a place *within* the first ten Wranglers by force of a
monstrous memory. A friend of mine was astonished
by his own confession that he got both his place and
his fellowship on the strength of that alone, and that
he could not solve an easy problem. "Here,"
said Mr. W——, handing my friend Airy's Tracts,
"do you just try me. Turn to any page you like,
and put me on at any line." The result was most
satisfactory; Airy's Tracts had been learnt by rote.

The Mathematical Tripos is not intended to meet
exceptional cases. It is a test of *working power*, and
nothing else; and a capital test it is. The expert can
there beat the genius; as in the cases of Griffin
and Sylvester, Parkinson and Thomson, Niven and
Clifford. Such are the only charges which have
ever been made against this happy institution; and
what is the guarantee, but the inflexible rule by which
the Examiners are chosen on their demonstrated
merits ?

In the Classical Tripos a similar rule prevails; but it
is somewhat flexible. Besides Fellows of King's, who
have distinguished themselves as University Scholars
or Prizemen, two gentlemen have served as Exa-

miners who have not taken Classical Honours—viz.
the late John Wordsworth, who was Porson Prizeman, and the Rev. J. J. S. Perowne, who was Junior
Bell's Scholar and Members' Prizeman. This Tripos
never suffered in disrepute but once, when an attempt
was made by an Examiner, a Fellow of Christ's, to
give unjust precedence to a member of his own college
over a Trinity man ; in which case the Examiner was
disgraced by a *non placet* when his candidature next
came before the Senate.

Now, the fact is, that no such custom regulates the
nomination or election of the Examiners of the Moral
Sciences Tripos. They are usually gentlemen distinguished for their Classics, their Mathematics, or
both ; rarely, and only exceptionally, distinguished,
either by their places in the Moral Sciences Tripos, or
by their published writings on any of the subjects of
the Tripos. To speak plainly, this matter may one
day become a grave scandal, throwing discredit on
the whole concern. It sounds passing strange and
well nigh incredible, and yet it is the fact, that since
the reconstruction of the Moral Sciences Tripos in
1861, only *five* graduates whose names are found in
that Tripos have officiated as its Examiners. This
looks like publishing to the world that the Tripos
has been a failure. The Board seem to be proclaim-
ing that the crop of philosophers and logicians it has
reared has been so light, or so poor, that very few
can be found, *even in its first classes*, to whom the
work of examination can be safely entrusted. The
only other interpretation is one that throws discredit
on the Board itself. The Board of Moral Sciences

Studies must accept one reading or the other. Probably they never troubled their heads on the matter; but their acts, in nominating Classics and Mathematicians, who have never given any public evidence of philosophical proficiency, to do the work in these examinations, cannot elude criticism, and even the most friendly criticism, if at all fair, cannot escape *both* interpretations.

Before the epoch of 1861 the Examiners were, *ex officio*, the Professors of Moral Philosophy, Political Economy, the Laws of England, and English History, with an additional Examiner for each year. During this initiatory decade forty-six names occur in the first classes, out of which it ought to have been easy to find competent Examiners for the next years. Easy or difficult, the task could not have been attempted. Only two of those forty-six have been Examiners since that epoch!

The following table, from which I have excluded the Professors of Moral Philosophy, whose office is the guarantee of their fitness, gives a complete list of the Examiners of the Moral Sciences Tripos from 1861 to 1869, showing the number of times each has served, and their places in the three Triposes. To this information I have added remarks on the public acts of those gentlemen in connection with philosophical or other subjects: as to which I can only regret that the facts I have obtained are so few. I think it is not impertinent to add, that not one of them, save Mr. Cope and Mr. Venn, is known to fame as a metaphysician or logician, though all are men of very great ability in other respects.

Name of Examiner	His College	Number of times he has served.	His place in the Math. Tripos.	His place in the Class. Tripos.	His place in the Mo. Sc. Tripos.	Remarks.
Campion, W. M.	Queen's	3	4 Wr.	S . Cl.	...	Author of "An Introduction to Arist. Rh.", "A Review of Aristotle's System of Ethics," and of "Plato's Theætetus and Mr. Grote's Criticisms"; also translator of Plato's Gorgias, &c.
Cope, E. M.	Trinity	1	15 Jun. Op.			Political Economist.
Courtney, L. H.	John's	2	2 Wr.			
Fuller, J.	Emmanuel	2	5 Wr.	a . 1		
Hammond, J. L.	Trinity	2	28 Wr.	a . 5	*I . 4	Moral Philosophy Prizeman, author of an Essay on Coleridge in the "Cambridge Essays."
Hort, F. J. A.	,,	3	33 Jun. Op.			
Mansel, S.	,,	1	...	a . 6	I . 2	Political Economist and littérateur.
Mayor, J. B.	John's	3	...	a . 2	*II . 2	Le Bas Prizeman, 1863, and littérateur.
Mozley, J. R.	King's	1	13 Wr.	a . 5	...	Poet and Essayist.
Myers, F. W. H.	Trinity	2	...	a . 3	I . 2	
Roby, H. J.	John's	1	...	S . Cl.		Littérateur.
Sidgwick, H.	Trinity	2	33 Wr.	S . Cl.		
Stephen, L.	Trin. Hall	3	20 Wr.			Voluminous mathematical author.
Todhunter, T.	John's	2	S. Wr.			Author of "The Logic of Chance," and Hulsean Lecturer, 1869.
Venn, J.	Caius	1	7 Wr.			
Webster, T.	Trinity	2	14 Jun. Op.	a . 5	*I . 1	Law Lecturer at Trinity College.
Westlake, J.	,,	2	7 Wr.	a . 6		

* Before 1861. I observe that in the table on page 29 the places in Mo: Sc: Tr: of Messrs. Droop and Webster are accidentally transposed. Mr. Shield's place, too, should be I. 2, instead of II. 1. To obviate misconception, I add, that it was only to the attack on the metaphysicians made (on the occasion referred to at the top of that page) by two eminent mathematicians, that I intended to apply the terms "acrimony and unfairness."

This table contains eleven first-classmen in Classics,
of whom four are Wranglers. It also contains six
Wranglers who did not go out in Classics. The
preponderance of classical men in this list is noticeable, and is explained by the fact that so much
of the examination turns on the Ancient History of
Philosophy, though that subject has been omitted
from the curriculum.

CHAPTER IV.

THE SELECTION OF TEXT-BOOKS, AND INDICATION OF THE COURSE OF STUDY.

AMONG the Rules of the Moral Sciences Tripos are the following:—

That the questions in all the departments shall be in part of a special kind, having reference to *books* on the subjects; and in part of a general kind, having reference to the *subjects* themselves. These latter questions may take the form of theses for essays.

That it shall be the duty of the Board to mark out lines of study in the several subjects before mentioned: and to publish a List of Books in relation to which questions shall be set; modifying the same from time to time as occasion shall require.

We are now concerned with the *books* recommended, and the "line of study" thereby prescribed; not with the special *subjects* thereby embraced. From the establishment of the Moral Sciences Tripos until the Grace of March 28, 1867, Jurisprudence and the History of Philosophy were (as I have said) included in the curriculum; but that grace did not take effect till the examination of 1869. Accordingly it is with the Revised List of Books, approved by the Senate

on that day, that we are chiefly concerned. This I
will now subjoin, pointing out, in parenthetical
remarks, the changes which this grace made in the
first list agreed to by the Board of Moral Sciences
Studies on May 25, 1860: in addition, I shall set
out the titles of those books which directly concern
the existing curriculum, but are no longer recommended by the Board.

LIST OF REVISED BOOKS APPROVED BY GRACE OF THE
SENATE, DATED MARCH 28, 1867.

1.—MORAL AND POLITICAL PHILOSOPHY.

Plato, Republic.
Aristotle, Ethics.
Cicero, De Officiis.
Butler, Three Sermons on Human Nature.
Kant, Einleitung in die ⎱ Summarised in 1860
Metaphysik der Sitten. ⎰ as " Kant's Ethical
Kant, Tugendlehre. ⎰ System."
Stewart, Philosophy of the Active and Moral
Powers of Man. (Books I., II.)
Whewell, Elements of Morality, including Polity.
*Bentham, Principles of Morals and Legislation,
and Principles of the Civil Code.

2.—MENTAL PHILOSOPHY.

Descartes, Discours de la Méthode (except physical
speculations).
Locke, Essay concerning Human Understanding
(except Book III.)

Cousin, Philosophie de Locke.
Cousin, Philosophie de Kant.
Hamilton, Lectures on Metaphysics.
*Ferrier, Institutes of Metaphysic.
*Bain, The Senses and the Intellect.

3.—Logic.

*Mansel, Prolegomena Logica.
Hamilton, Lectures on Logic.
Whately, Elements of Logic.
Thomson, Laws of Thought.
Bacon, Novum Organon (meaning his N. Organum).
Whewell, Novum Organon Renovatum.
Mill, System of Logic.

4.—Political Economy.

Adam Smith, Wealth of Nations.
Ricardo, Philosophy of Political Economy and Taxation.
Mill, Principles of Political Economy.
*Cairnes, Character and Logical Method of Political Economy.
*Bastiat, Harmonies Économiques.
Those books marked * were not in the list of 1860.

The following books were agreed to on March 25, 1860, but discontinued in 1867 :—

1.—Moral Philosophy.

Plato, The Moral Dialogues.
Cicero, De Finibus.

Clarke, On the Attributes, and on Unchangeable Morality.

Paley's Moral and Political Philosophy.

Whewell's Lectures on the History of Moral Philosophy.

Fichte's Ethical System (translated works, Vol. I.)

2.—MENTAL PHILOSOPHY.

Plato's Theætetus.

Aristotle, De Anima.

Reid's Philosophy (Hamilton's Notes and Dissertations).

Kant's Kritik der reinen Vernunft (In Bohn's Series).

Cousin's Philosophe du XVIII. Siècle. [The parts relating to Locke and Kant retained.]

3.—LOGIC.

Aristotle's Categories and Analytics.

Trendelenburg's Elementa Logices Aristotelicæ.

Aldrich, with Mansel's Notes.

4.—POLITICAL ECONOMY.

The works of Malthus, McCulloch, Jones, Carey, and Chevallier.

Both lists are faulty in their very nature. A general direction is of very little use to students, especially in respect to authors that are not "familiar in their mouths as household words." Greater precision should have been observed in specifying

the particular works recommended. Supposing the
Board to have had an adequate knowledge both of
subjects and of books, they should, as a rule, have
specified *editions*, and recommended particular *translations*. As it is, the Revised List, like its prede-
cessor, is loose and slovenly, and mainly of use for the
direction of the Examiners. The changes introduced
into it are on the whole judicious, though some of
them are quite the reverse. In Moral Philosophy, the
substitution of Bentham for Fichte is unfortunate on
all grounds. In Mental Philosophy, to banish Kant's
Critic of the Pure Reason, the head and source of all
that is worthy of the name of Philosophy, and to
retain the feeble, dilute, and often most erroneous
exposition of Cousin, was an act of sheer fatuity and
ignorance, which no policy can excuse. The selec-
tions in Logic and Political Economy are commend-
able. It *is* difficult to select without a standard: and
evidently this is what the Board found themselves
under the necessity of doing.

"Whether any given Mathematical work," writes
Whewell, in his tract, *Of a Liberal Education in
General*, 1845, p. 69, "can properly be distinguished
as one of the capital works of the subject, is a matter
to be decided by the general and permanent judgment of the mathematical world." He does not say
how long we are to wait for that œcumenical verdict,
nor what we are to do in the meantime. As to
Mathematics, the verdict has long since been returned. The list it sanctions is well known ; and an
adequate selection from it is given by Whewell at

page 66 of that little work. Now I candidly confess, that in the present stage of philosophical development it is impossible to select text-books for the Moral Sciences Tripos by such an appeal. But it is, surely, self-evident that a work in any department of science must *be* a sound *objective* treatise before it can be *such* "by the general and permanent judgment of the [philosophical] world." There must always be a time when the minority of that world are right, and the majority wrong. It is always so: the less is more than the greater, before the greater is more than the less : a paradox of which the history of science affords a continual series of examples in point. The crystal spheres of George Purbach remained triumphant, distracting and perplexing the students of every European Academy, long after their doom had been sealed by the tranquil Monk of Thorn. The Vortices of Descartes maintained their ascendancy in every French College for fifty years after the promulgation of Newton's *Principia.* Yet, in neither case do we pretend that the new had not virtually superseded the old at the moment of innovation. Every *objective* treatise must win its way to the acceptance of the *subjectivities*, whose congruent opinions will thereafter, not through the worth of opinion, but by the weight of congruence, be the test of its fitness to serve as a basis of education.

Next to the banishment of Kant's great work in favour of his commentator Cousin, the retention of certain books, and the absence of others, are points calculated to provoke the gravest dissatisfaction. It

E

is no dislike of empirical psychology that induces
me to single out from the list Professor Bain's
work on *The Senses and the Intellect* for special
blame. Whatever may be its merits, it is, *me
judice*, quite unfit to serve as a text-book; nor is
any one of those formidable bales of mental goods, of
which he is the reputed packer, to be recommended
to the student as either wholesome or useful. The
plan upon which they are compiled is as simple as it
is useless. Professor Bain finds in his mind some
schema of his subject ; what it is he does not reveal ;
but from this he selects a form of classification, according to which he amasses his undigested materials,
and the result is not a treatise, but a *cento*. In this
proceeding he follows, but with more daring and less
shrewdness, the lead of Mr. J. S. Mill. His end
appears to be, to furnish forth the concrete materials
of his subject in the minutest detail, and yet with the
utmost economy of particular expression, while the
theory, which alone could afford the excuse for this
ostentation of facts, is confined to his own consciousness. In these days of learned display and intellectual
poverty, such books obtain for their authors great re-
pute. Whilst I demur to the popular verdict in this
regard, I am quite aware that it is not in my power to
disturb it. I may, indeed, *hope* that my voice may be
heard at the Board of Moral Sciences Studies, and
that *The Senses and the Intellect* may be struck off the
list. But I am not so sanguine as to *expect* this
result ; and should not be astonished if the candidates for Honours were to be further abused by the

addition of another of Professor Bain's works to
the prescribed books of the Tripos. Whilst I am
writing this censure, my attention is called to a
review of his last work—his *Logic*—in the *Edinburgh
Evening Courant*, April 19, 1870, from which I make
a short extract in support of what I have said :—

" In his various writings, Professor Bain does not so much
provide us with the *tree* of knowledge as, so to speak, with its
bush. The tree he seems to keep to himself, and for his own
private purposes. Bush they are or scrub—immitigable scrub.
How we wander in them, lost, lifting weary foot after weary
foot, without the slightest glimpse of cessation—of any outlet
anywhere ! Did any mortal—not peculiarly compelled thereto
—ever read any one of them through ? Did any mortal, who at
any time did read in them, not find himself waking up from
vacancy to ask—' What is this ? Have I got a single idea, a
single particle of information out of all this ? Clear sentences,
yes ; but what is in them, and what is the effect of the whole ?
Why, nightmare!' Movements, sensations, discriminations, assi-
milations, recurrences, emotions, volitions. Well, that is the
subjective side, and all beaten on his tree into absolute inanity.
But even then, when we are trembling in his clutch with
very nervousness, he seems to thank a bountiful Providence
for enabling him to detain us actually twice as long yet—
with the objective side ; the same tree is applied to the
whole outward, and everything in heaven and on earth,
whether of work-day or feast-day distinction, whether common or illustrious—trade, commerce, art, science, literature,
government, what not, endlessly—is intruded on our attention
with a pertinacity of insistence which, in exact proportion to
the sober dulness of the material, needs only the addition of
perception of the sober self-complacency of the writer to
achieve at length our utter and complete prostration.
These are unpleasant experiences, but, as recorded on our
part, they are perfectly true and honest ones. Nevertheless,
we cannot say that the reading of the work before us was
attended by all of them, and in the same degree. To us, at
least, Mr. Bain's *Logic* is not as heavy as his *Senses and
Intellect*, or his *Emotions and Will* ; certainly not by a great

E 2

many degrees as heavy as that bog, named *Compendium of Psychology and Ethics*, into which it has been his will recently to plunge both works together hopelessly out of sight."

Every word of this is as true as the Gospel; yet this *Compendium*, crude and indigest beyond its fellows, this morass, which has absorbed in its quaking bulk two of its predecessors, deserves some praise for its *Appendix*. Among the many fables told of the beaver is that which concerns the functions of its tail. That appendage is said to possess a medicinal virtue, as well as to serve its owner as truck and trowel; and I have somewhere read that it has been known, when pursued by the dogs, to bite off its tail, and leave it, as a trophy, to its pursuers. Happy would the students of Bain's *Compendium* be, if its tail should remain in their hands, after the useless trunk had escaped to the burrow of oblivion.*

---

* It is the rumour in London, that the most valuable sections of this *Appendix* were written by Mr. Grote. I heard this asserted by one who had the best means of knowing its truth. De Quincey gives an amusing account of Coleridge's everlasting praise of Ball and Bell, Bell and Ball, in perplexing reiteration. I find the general public are similarly perplexed by Bain and Baynes; and now that each is a Scotch Professor, and a logical author and editor, the confusion will be worse confounded. The late Bishop Phillpotts used to speak of the Bishop of Worcester as his "singular brother." Let it be clearly understood that my strictures do not concern Professor Baynes, whose *New Analytic of Logical Forms* and translation of the *Port Royal Logic* are works of great merit. He is, in some important respects, an abler man than his "singular brother," whatever may be the state of public opinion on the matter. The former of these works also contains so valuable an *Appendix* on the History of Logic as to justify its addition to the Revised List of Books.

Locke's *Essay*, too, might also be spared. It is obsolete, besides being in the last degree cumbersome and perplexing to the student. Yet, in view of the History of Philosophy, he may well, *ex abundanti cautelâ*, have recourse to select portions of the *Essay*. The omissions are more serious. In the first place Hume's philosophical works ought to be included. His relation to Kant is even more important than that of Fichte; for it is necessary to understand Hume, in order to appreciate the initiatory step of Kant; whereas Fichte is required, rather as an outcome of Kant, than as a preparation for Hegel. On this relation of Hume and Kant, Dr. J. H. Stirling has written with even more than his usual felicity of expression. Here is his *dictum* :—

"Hume, with infinite fertility, surprised us, it may be said, perhaps, into attention on a great variety of points which had hitherto passed unquestioned ; but, even on these points, his success was of an interrupted, scattered, and inconclusive nature. He set the world adrift, but he set man too, reeling and miserable, adrift with it. Kant again, with gravity and reverence, desired to refix, but in purity and truth, all those relations and institutions which alone give value to existence— which alone *are* humanity, in fact—but which Hume, with levity and mockery, had approached to shake. Kant built up again an entire new world for us of knowledge and duty, and, in a certain way, even belief; whereas Hume had sought to dispossess us of every support that man as man could hope to cling to. In a word, with *at least* equal fertility, Kant was, as compared with Hume, a graver, deeper, and, so to speak, a more consecutive, more comprehensive spirit. Graces there were indeed, or even, it may be, subtleties, in which Hume had the advantage, perhaps. He is still in England an unsurpassed master of expression—this, certainly, in his History, if in his Essays he somewhat baffles his own self by a certain laboured breadth of conscious fine writing, often singularly inexact and infelicitous. Still Kant, with reference to his products, must be allowed much the greater importance. In the history of Philosophy he will probably always command as influential a place in the modern world as Socrates in the ancient; while as probably Hume will occupy at best some such position as that of Heraclitus or Protagoras." (*As RegardsProtoplasm*, 1869, pp. 4 and 5.)

According to my judgment, Hume is the only author before Kant with whom the student of Modern Philosophy has any *need* to be conversant. Locke, Condillac, Leibnitz, Berkeley, and Wolff may be dispensed with. Accordingly, Hume's *Treatise on Human Nature*, and his *Essays*, should be added to the Revised List. New editions of both, by Messrs. T. H. Green, and T. H. Grose, of Balliol College, Oxford, are at press, and will shortly be published by Longmans & Co.

There is but one portal to Modern Philosophy, and but one key to Ancient Philosophy; that portal is Kant, and that key is furnished by the greatest outcome of Kant's Philosophy, viz. Hegel. I am not disposed to dogmatise on these matters. I assert a self-evident fact, that for the advanced student of Metaphysics no other door stands open. To employ Dr. Stirling's figure of speech, no teacher that comes after Kant should be listened to, unless it be certified that he has emptied Kant's vessel into his own.

No other philosophy, but what derives from Kant, explains for us the source of *apodeictic judgments*. Many writers deny that we have such, unless they are truisms. To Cambridge men such writers waste their breath. Kant's sole aim and end was to account for this fact, that we make apodeictic judgments on matters whereof the reality is empirical. Clearly, whatever a system of Mental Philosophy may do, it is *false* if it deny those judgments; it is *useless* if it fail to account for them. No other philosophy, but what derives from Kant, explains for us the nature of *unconditioned obligation*. Many writers deny that we have such. May that time be far distant, nay, may Cambridge be a lichened ruin ere the day dawn, when the learning she has fostered shall shake the dominion of Immutable Morality and Religious Faith. Equally clearly, whatever a system of Moral Philosophy may be, it is an *iniquity* if it ignore unconditioned obligation; it is an *impertinence* if it fail to systematise it.

The paramount value of Kant's Speculative Philosophy was not overlooked by Whewell. He founded upon Kant: some say foundered. I know not any English writer who has attempted to expound or popularise Kant that has not, at one time or another, been accused of making a "stumble at the threshold," of misconceiving some doctrine, or of misunderstanding some technicality. Such charges fell as light as snow-flakes on the Platonic shoulders of Whewell. Stumbled every student has, and every expert was a student once. Most, to speak truly, never get beyond the threshold, and ought to think themselves very fortunate if they can live in the rarefied air and dry light of the Categories. A complete catalogue of such stumbles, gathered in from Coleridge, Hamilton, Whewell, Lewes, Mansel,

&c., if it could be done in all sweetness and ἐπιείκεια, so as not to wound the feelings of the most sensitive, would be a welcome help to students and a good in itself, serving both for present guidance and for future history. My own contribution should be at the service of such a work; for, happily, one may speak of a difficulty surmounted, without shame, and without rebuke. The chief hindrance to the realisation of this project would be occasioned by those who have mistaken the way, and journeyed on too far to retrace their steps without some shame and inconvenience. The meanings of a *transcendental* deduction; of a *synthetical* judgment; of the *intuition* of Space and Time; of the functions of *apperception* (*i.e.* the Categories), &c. &c., have been very generally mistaken and misstated. Whewell has a few sins of the kind to answer for. He owed somewhat to Kant; but in no way can he be considered, any more than Coleridge, a guide to Kant. He, like Coleridge, was too deficient in recipiency to serve such a purpose; and, unlike Coleridge, he was quite insufficient in subtlety to make a philosopher. Truth to say, he had a lurking dislike and suspicion of Metaphysics, and this is unconsciously manifested in all his attempts to weld the Natural Philosophy of England with the Metaphysics, or Philosophy proper, of Germany. An example will not be out of place here. He taught that the proposition, "The pressure on the fulcrum is equal to the sum of the weights," was an axiom of mechanics, a necessary, self-evident truth. Nothing could come of such

blundering as that. What else can it be called ?
First, the proposition (with its necessary qualification)
is not an axiom at all; but a theorem, admitting of,
and requiring, proof; and, *Secondly*, the proposition,
read quite *trocken*, is false. The necessary qualification is, as Hamilton pointed out (*Discussions*,
1852, p. 324), "together with the weight of the
lever." The omission of that was an oversight, the
fruit of that carelessness which gave our late Master
so much trouble, and so little concern. But let it
be given in, as a subaudition. Well, what then ?
Why, then, as De Morgan showed (*Formal Logic*,
1847, p. 180), the truth of the proposition is, indeed,
unquestionable, but only as a deduction from the
law of action and reaction; for the upward and
downward attractions of the weights and the respec-
tive parts of the lever have to be taken into consideration, and it is found that they exactly balance
each other.

That which goes under the name of philosophy,
in Whewell, is indeed a miserable and attenuated
fragment. It consists in the assertion and illustration of a few necessary and inseparable antitheses,
such as Fact and Idea, and in stating and exem-
plifying their correlations. "Knowledge requires
ideas. Reality requires things." These with Whewell
were ultimate truths! The Master, bred in a mixed
atmosphere of Scholasticism and Mathematics, and
subsequently trained (some say very inadequately)
in Physics, thought it no impertinence in himself
to opine that on a matter, which had occupied the

greatest intellects in the world, there was nothing
to be discovered. He did not declare the complete
or ultimate explanation of such correlations to be
impossible, as others with greater assurance and
less knowledge have done, but that it " appears to
be beyond our reach." De Morgan, like Whewell,
allows the fact that we do exercise apodeictic
judgments, (and in these days of empiricism, we
ought to be thankful for so small a mercy,) but
adds, " Why a judgment is apodeictic, it is not
within our power to say." (*Formal Logic*, 1847, p. 33.)
It is but fair to read that assertion as a personal
confession ; *quasi dicat, nostro judicio.* To take it
otherwise would amount to an imputation on his self-
knowledge ; for De Morgan never pretended to have
mastered Kant, still less to have ascended to a higher
tower of speculation, and to have superseded Kant's
Transcendental Science by Transcendent Nescience.
The simple fact is, Kant's *force* has never been
excelled, and his *scope* has never been enlarged by
any but Hegel. No other man's *horizon* has ever
reduced Kant's to a *foreground*. No other author has
ever swallowed up Kant, and reproduced him in the
form of new tissue. To Hamilton or Mansel, or any
other herbivorous feeder, who, having sniffed at
some of Kant's *orts*, pretends that he has done that
feat, the great sage may borrow the geologist's
reply to the ramping and roaring owner of the " tail,
horns and hoofs "—

" You know you *can't* eat ME !
Why—you're a ruminating graminivorous animal !"

Just as soon should we believe that an ox had devoured a lion.

Whewell, then, is, as I have said, no guide at all to Kant. His fundamental position is essentially different from Kant's. To Whewell the *matter* presented to the senses is a thing in itself; to Kant a *phenomenon*. Accordingly Whewell, whether he stumbled at the threshold or not, most assuredly did not get beyond the threshold, and little threshing of any sort did he do there: so that his philosophy is of the smallest. Such as it is, it is in logical, if not vital, connection with the physical edifice he reared upon it; and his positions are taken with such clearness, and illustrated with such fulness, that I for one should be glad to see his *History of Scientific Ideas* and a portion of his *Philosophy of Discovery* included in the Revised List of the Moral Sciences Tripos, as it already is in that of the Natural Sciences Tripos. In the presence of Whewell's three works, Mill's Logic might be struck off the list. Of course Kant's three *Kritiken* should be added to it. In reading the first, the student might consult Mr. Meiklejohn's English version of that work, and a portion of the third translated by the late Mr. Semple in his version of Kant's *Metaphysic of Ethics*, will be considerable use. In addition, the list should include Kant's *Religion innerhalb den Grenzen der bloszen Vernunft*, of which, also, a fair version was published by Mr. Semple. (Copies of both of Mr. Semple's translations may be had of Messrs. T. & T. Clark, Edinburgh.)

The History of Philosophy is, of course, an indispensable study; but, for some reason which I cannot divine, the subject is no longer *expressly* included in the curriculum, the Second Rule of May 24, 1859, having been annulled on May 25, 1860. However, as questions on the History are still set, the List of Books ought (if only to avoid stultification) to include some work on that subject. It would be too much to ask every student to take the pains of Mr. Norman Maccoll, who, for his excellent Hare Prize Essay, 1868, had recourse to Hegel's *Lectures*, the *Histories of Philosophy* of Ritter, Brandis, Schwegler, Erdmann, and Zeller, as well as Prantl's *History of Logic*. We have in English a considerable assortment of such works, original and translated. For the purposes of the Moral Sciences Tripos, I should give the preference to Schwegler's *Handbook of Philosophy*, translated by Dr. J. H. Stirling. The annotations, by Dr. Stirling, are fully as important as the text of the work, and are almost of equal bulk.

Schwegler's *Handbook* is not only indispensable, but sufficient; still I may as well indicate here what is our *matériel* in this regard. Besides the Histories of Dr. J. D. Morell and Mr. Robert Blakey, there are several translated works of merit. Foremost of these are the three volumes of Zeller's *History of the Philosophy of the Greeks*, two of which have been translated for us by the Rev. O. J. Reichel, Vice Principal of Cuddesden College, viz. *Socrates and the Socratic Schools*, and *The Stoics, Epicureans, and Sceptics;* the translation of the intermediate volume, viz.

Aristotle and the Later Peripatetics, by Mr. John Addington Symonds, of Queen's College, Oxford, being at press. Another book of sterling value is a volume of Professor Kuno Fischer's *History of Modern Philosophy*, translated into English by Mr. J. P. Mahaffy, Fellow and Tutor of Trinity College, Dublin. It is entitled *A Commentary on Kant's Critick of the Pure Reason*. All these four works are published by Longmans & Co.

I cannot recommend the *Historical Survey of Speculative Philosophy from Kant to Hegel*, by Professor H. M. Chalybäus. However, for those who care to possess it in English, I may say that it has been twice translated, viz. by the Rev. Alfred Edersheim, formerly of Aberdeen, now Professor in the University of Kiel (Edinburgh, T. & T. Clark, 1853), and Mr. Alfred Tulk (Longmans & Co. 1854). Both versions are said, on good authority, to be excellent.

Schwegler's *Handbook* has also been translated, in the United States of America, by Mr. Seelye. He used the first edition ; while Dr. Stirling more wisely translated the more accurate fifth edition of that work.

The addition of Hegel to the list will sooner or later be inevitable, but I hesitate to advise it, for want of an elementary text-book of the Hegelian system, intelligible to advanced students. Those, however, who have struggled with Kant may with advantage attack Dr. J. H. Stirling's *Secret of Hegel*, 2 vols., Longmans & Co., 1865, which contains a translation of the *Logic*, with an ample commen-

tary on both the *Quality* and the *Quantity*. But,
apart from Hegel, that splendid work affords the only
trustworthy English commentary on Kant. For the
sake of the third and fifth chapters alone, *The Secret of
Hegel* should be added to the Revised List.

In this chapter I have been particular in mention-
ing translations from Greek and German authors.
What I have written has been prompted by the
strongest conviction of the great utility of reading
their works in English.

" The respectable and sometimes excellent translations of
Bohn's Library," writes Emerson (*Society and Solitude, Essay
on Books*), "have done for literature what railroads have done
for internal intercourse. . . . . The Italians have a
fling at translators,—*i traditori traduttori;* but I thank them.
I rarely read any Latin, Greek, German, Italian, sometimes
not a French book, in the original, which I can procure in a
good version. I like to be beholden to the great metropolitan
English speech, the sea which receives tributaries from every
region under heaven. I should as soon think of swimming
across Charles river, when I wish to go to Boston, as of
reading all my books in originals, when I have them rendered for me in my mother tongue."

Yet on the other hand, in studying a special
philosophical system, the translation is never quite
enough, the original never wholly dispensable. In
general literature Emerson's assertions hold good
with little or no qualification. Dr. Newman, speaking of classical scholarship, writes on this wise
(*Grammar of Assent*, 1870, p. 20) :—

" Hence in literary examinations it is a test of good
scholarship to be able to construe aright, without the aid of
understanding the sentiment, action, or historical occurrence
conveyed in the passage thus accurately rendered, let it be a

battle in Livy, or some subtle train of thought in Virgil or Pindar. And those who have acquitted themselves best in the trial, will often be disposed to think they have most notably failed, for the very reason that they have been too busy with the grammar of each sentence, as it came, to have been able, as they construed on, to enter into the facts or the feelings, which, unknown to themselves, they were bringing out of it."

But the case of a difficult philosophical author is quite different from those contemplated by the gifted Oratorian. A Greek or German word and its English synonym may be compared, as was done by De Quincey, to two intersecting circles, the common area being the basis of exact interpretation, the other areas containing the sources of misprision. But the primary and derivative meanings of a word in the original may go to make up the entire extent and intent which it stood to cover; while the English equivalent not only excludes some of those meanings, but connotes others that are impertinent: and in the statement of a philosophical system *exactitude* of expression is the *sinon non.*

But, while allowing the full force of this view of the case, it is, nevertheless, true, that very few students acquire such familiarity with Greek or German, or in fact *any* foreign tongue, dead or living, as to read a difficult work in that language with the same facility of comprehension as they read an English book. Hence arises the imperative necessity of using an English translation alongside of the German or Greek text. In fact, it hardly appears as if the best scholarship is sufficient for the full understanding of Aristotle or Plato.

The finest scholars of my own College were, not many years ago, divided as to the meaning of a passage in the *Posterior Analytics*, Book II.; one side contended that the words πᾶν ἄχολον contained a textual error, the other were for giving a special interpretation to the traditional text. A well-known scholar "nourished on mood and figure in the cloisters of Oxford" was called in to arbitrate between the disputants. He summarily disallowed the surgery contemplated by the one party, and as summarily rejected the diagnosis attempted by the other. He showed them that πᾶν ἄχολον was necessary to the vital sense of the passage according to which the Stagirite was expounding a special kind of syllogism applicable to Induction only. The Cambridge scholarship was great; but the intelligence was inversely proportional to the scholarship.

The remedy for such a state of things lies in a judicious use of translations.

CHAPTER V.

THE papers set in the past eighteen examinations
are now mere things of the past, which have no
interest for any one but the critic of the Tripos; of
course, I never dreamed of attempting so quixotic a
proceeding as unearthing a mass of papers, which
might constitute a ponderous blue-book, in order to
make them the basis of an exhaustive criticism. In
fact, I have seen only the examination-papers of 1868
and 1869, and even these are far too voluminous for
my purpose. Those of 1868 were founded on the
Rules and superseded List of 1860, while those of
1869 belong to the first year of the Rules and Revised
List of 1867 ; so that, together, they form a sufficient
representative of the entire system. Having selected
these papers, there still remained the task of select-
ing subjects or questions. As a preliminary, I determined to dismiss from consideration the History of
Philosophy, General Jurisprudence, and Political
Philosophy ; the two former being no longer a part
of the curriculum, and the latter but a subordinate
and unessential part of Moral Philosophy. On a
review of the residue, composing the essentials of the
last subject, Mental Philosophy. Political Economy

and Logic, I could see no occasion for occupying space with either Political Economy, or Logic; for the papers in both seemed to me, on the whole, satisfactory, showing an adequate knowledge in the questioners, and being well calculated to test that of the questionists. So far forth I felt that the conductors of this Tripos were to be congratulated on having done their work remarkably well.

I therefore propose to comment on a few of the questions in Moral and Mental Philosophy; and these shall be such as belong to Modern Philosophy; for not only is the German movement the most important in the entire History of Philosophy, but it is the works of French, English and German authors, rather than those of the Greeks and Romans, that promise a satisfactory test of the Examiners' knowledge and capability. It would surprise me to find them tripping in Plato; it would surprise me more if they did not trip in Kant.

But, in the first place, taking these papers as a whole, I must say that greater strictness in the distribution of questions should have been observed. For instance, we find in the papers of 1868, in Mental Philosophy, two questions which certainly belong to Logic, viz :—

"Explain clearly the chief uses and abuses of language. Show, with examples, how apparent disputes about words are often really disputes about things."

"Explain distinctly, with examples, how far and on what grounds etymology is a safe guide to the meaning of an abstract term. Give the rationale of other means of interpretation. Show which must ultimately be the supreme authority."

On the other hand, we find in those of 1869, in Logic, two questions which as certainly belong to Mental Philosophy, viz. :—

"Explain the dispute between Mansel and Mill on Mathematical Necessity. Why can we not conceive that two straight lines should enclose a space ? Is this an Analytical or a Synthetical Judgment ?" [Which ?]

"It is often [*sic*] said that two and two make four. Is this an identical proposition or a definition of the word 'four' ? Or does it express a truth recognised by intuition, or arrived at as the result of experience ? Is it in any sense inconceivable that two and two should make five ?"

Again, we find in the papers of 1869, in Mental Philosophy, one question which, in strictness, should have been classed with those in Moral Philosophy, viz. :—

"'Liberty cannot be an attribute of the will.' What does Locke mean by this statement ? Compare his opinion on this subject with that of Mill."

I observe, too, a want of proportion in these papers. Unimportant authors are too prominent : leading constructive minds are slighted or ignored ; and this quite irrespective of the presence of either in the Revised List. Everywhere we see a preponderance of History (or Philosophical Biography) over Philosophy proper. The Rules, indeed, do not provide against it, and in this they are right ; for it is a matter in which the Examiners should be left unshackled. But their common sense should have told them that the science is the first requirement, and the literature of the science a quite secondary, if not indifferent, matter. Take for illustration the case of a mathematical examination (as that for Smith's Prizes) : what would be thought if the Examiners should ask such a question as this :—

" State and discuss Professor Tait's views on Sir William Rowan Hamilton's curt refutation of the differential theory of Lagrange in the T. R. I. A."

Yet in the papers of 1869, in Mental Philosophy, the following question is proposed :—

" Explain and discuss Cousin's assertion that Leibnitz was the first to seize the weak side of Cartesianism. In what respects, if any, do you consider Leibnitz to have contributed to the sound progress of philosophy ?"

Surely that is *de trop*. Who is the better for knowing that Cousin rejoiced in a certain critique of Leibnitz on a particular doctrine of Descartes ? It is bad enough for a student to have to get up the critique of Leibnitz on a point where Descartes and Leibnitz are wholly and irrecoverably superseded. There is too much of this in these papers, *e.g.* What are Hamilton's views on Descartes, and on Bacon ? What is Whewell's critique on Bentham ? What is Cousin's critique on Locke ? &c. &c. The student in the Moral Sciences cannot do everything ; and surely the minor details of the history of Philosophy should not be allowed to occupy a prominent place in these examinations.

One other point, and I conclude these preliminary strictures. The papers of 1869 have a glut of what may be called technological questions : for instance we have the following in Moral Philosophy :—

" Distinguish the following terms :—*liberty, power, action, will, volition, intention, inclination, disposition, wish, desire, resolution, firmness, obstinacy.*"

And the following in Mental Philosophy :—

" Explain the following terms :—*Substratum, Mode, Proper, Sensible, Sensus Communis, Pre-established Harmony, Forms of Consciousness, Presentation and Representation, Cosmothetic Idealism.*"

The papers of 1868 contrast favourably with their successors in this respect. At this rate the examination will result in imposing on the candidates the requirement of compiling a philosophical dictionary. The extraordinary hodge-podge of puerilities in some of these questions cannot be read without laughter, reminding one of De Morgan's skit on a passage in Mr. S. Warren's *Diary of a Late Physician,* which would make a capital question in Latin Grammar : viz.—

" Explain the following terms :—*Propria quæ maribus ; botherum ; tempus fugit ; hic, hæc, hoc ; nominativo.*"—(*Notes and Queries. 2nd Series, xii. 237.*)

" Nun lasst uns zu unserer Aufgabe fortgehen," as Kant says, after a tedious prelusion. Of the three operations, setting a paper for examination, working it for marks, and criticising it on its merits, the last alone is thankless, and that presents the greatest difficulty. The criticism is twofold : it has to determine the efficiency of the Examiner, and the efficacy of the paper ; it has to answer two questions : (1) How far is the paper calculated to try the knowledge of the candidates ? (2) How far does it certify the knowledge of the Examiner in the subject of which it treats? and there are the residual questions, whether that subject is suitable for the occasion, and, if so, whether it is treated at a length, or with a detail, disproportionate to other subjects of higher claims. Clearly, a question which betrays the ignorance of the Examiner can only by a lucky chance serve the purpose of the examination. Equally plain is it that, as a test of the candidates' proficiency, the questions must be taken as evidence of the kind of knowledge that is required of them. If nearly half a paper consist of questions on Cicero (as was actually the case in 1869), it must be presumed that the Examiners attach a proportionable value to the works of that author. If there are, say, ten questions on Cicero to one on Kant, in a paper in Moral Philosophy, I should infer that the questioner considers the *De Officiis* and *De Finibus* ten times more valuable than the *Kritik der praktischen Vernunft* and the *Metaphysik der Sitten!* One can only make a note of admiration and pass on.

Questions which eschew particularisation of a doctrine, on which something is demanded, and those which give, in that regard, the *ipsissima verba* of the author, can testify nothing as to the Examiner's comprehension. On the other hand, those questions which require the student to expound or elucidate an express doctrine of a particular author, without giving it *in verba magistri*, may bear witness for or against the Examiner. Of course, either, indifferently, may be good searching questions for the examinees, or the reverse, as the case may be.

To take a hypothetical example : if I were to set the following question :—

" ' Kant will not affirm the existence of a real space external to our minds.' Explain and discuss this allegation of Sir W. S. Hamilton's."

On this the critic may, indeed, question Hamilton's knowledge of Kant; but he cannot question my knowledge of Hamilton, for those are Hamilton's very words.

Again : if I were to set this question :—

"Kant says, 'The things we perceive are not, in themselves, what we take them for, nor their relations so constituted in themselves, as they appear to us.' Does this statement justify Mansel in saying, that here Kant ' contradicts his own fundamental hypothesis ' ? "

On this the critic may possibly (but unwisely) except to the translation of Kant's own words ; but, admitting the passage to be correctly rendered, he cannot impugn my knowledge either of Kant or of Mansel : for I do not commit myself to a single gloss on either.

But if, on the other hand, I propose this question:—

" ' From the Categories alone no synthetical proposition can be made.' Reconcile this assertion of Kant's with the doctrine of the *Critic*, that all synthesis is derived, *a priori*, from the Categories."

Now here the critic, while he cannot impugn my knowledge of Kant as to the assertion quoted *verbatim*, may put me on my trial as to the doctrine which I have ventured to summarise. This is the test I propose to apply to the papers of 1868 and 1869 in the two selected subjects.

I find there but *thirty* questions (out of about a hundred) containing express doctrines attributed to particular authors. Of these, *nine* only dispense with marks of quotation (inverted commas, or italics), and give the statement, with more or less freedom, from the Examiner's point of view. Here are the nine expressions of doctrine, two in Moral and seven in Mental Philosphy :—

SUMMARY OF DOCTRINE.	Attributed to
A conflict between utility and virtue is impossible ...	Cicero.
Moral Philosophy may take the form of a theory either of Duty, or of Virtue, or of Good	Schleiermacher.
The mind has perceptions independent of the organs of sensation	Plato.
True opinion is not knowledge	Plato.
A sensuous intuition is necessarily true	Epicurus.
Matter does not exist	Berkeley.
Space is a condition of our minds, not existing in the objects we behold	Kant.
Experience is the first product of the understanding ...	Kant.
The fundamental controversy of philosophy was waged between the efficient and the final cause	Trendelenburg.

There are but three of these attributions which can be disputed : viz. those which concern Berkeley and Kant. On strict inquiry, however, it will be found that the Examiners' positions are unassailable, save in one case ; and there they are demonstrably, and indeed culpably, wrong in the attempted summary of doctrine.

Of Kant's predecessors in modern times, whose works are not included in the Revised List, Berkeley, Reid, Leibnitz, Spinosa, and Hartley, and of his successors, Coleridge and Mr. Herbert Spencer, are mediately or immediately brought on the scene; Berkeley and Leibnitz playing, as was meet, the principal parts. In fact, if the papers are open to exception on the score of *range*, as opposed to *thoroughness*, I would say that their range is historically exorbitant, and a stricter limitation of authors would have been a great improvement. But I must waive the further consideration of the lesser lights in the philosophical firmament, and what I shall further say will be restricted to Berkeley and Kant: and on these I shall speak with the utmost condensation.

The test, then, by which I am to try the issue which respects the competency of the Examiners is (fortunately for my space) remarkably brief, consisting of one question on Berkeley and two on Kant. The former is in these terms :—

"Explain accurately Berkeley's denial of the existence of matter. 'There is nothing easier than to imagine trees in a park or books in a closet, and nobody by to perceive them.' What account does (1) Berkeley, (2) Mill, give of this belief that objects exist independently of our perception of them ? " —*Mental Philosophy*, 1869.

The adoption here of the vulgar belief of "Berkeley's denial of the existence of matter," would certainly be objected to by Messrs. Fraser and Simon; but, even if inaccurate, I am quite prepared to justify it in this connection: for the very object of the question is to invite the student to clear up an intentional ambiguity; so that, regarded in this light, we may see in it an evidence of the Examiners' intelligence and tact. After all, it is by no means to be allowed that the expression, "denial of the existence of matter," is an inaccuracy. It admits equally of justification and of refutation, according as it is read. Berkeley's *percipi* was *esse*; and the matter which he denies as an externality, which affects us as one external independent object does another, he admits as an internality affecting us *within*. Nevertheless, this very coadequation of perception and existence perceived, does practically amount to denying the objective existence of the very thing which the vulgar understand by the term *matter*. To the student, who knows the theory of Berkeley, and "the effects of his writings upon subsequent speculation" (asked for, together with his debts and originalities, elsewhere) the question must have been welcome. He doubtless availed himself of the occasion to exhibit both readings of the doctrine, and of entering on a consideration of the serious-looking objection, that Berkeley first assumes matter to be an externality, in order to reduce its qualities to a pure subjectivity, and then, from the subjectivity of those qualities, proves matter to be a mere internality: thus sawing through the plank he is bestriding. Here, too, the student had a rare chance of exposing Mr. J. S.

Mill's misrepresentation of Berkeley's argument (*Logic*, 1843, vol. ii. p. 451). Instead of quoting Berkeley's words, which would not have furnished Mr. Mill with the leverage he wanted, he gives his own summary of the argument, and, perhaps consciously, makes it absurd and ridiculous, while, certainly unintentionally, he utterly perverts it.*

We now proceed to consider the two questions on Kant. They are respectively in the papers of 1868 and 1869 in Mental Philosophy :—

"How does Kant answer the objection that by treating Space as a condition of our minds, not as existing in the objects we behold, he makes all phenomena illusory?"

An objection answered by Kant himself should be

---

* Only a few pages earlier, Mr. Mill serves up in the same amusing, but reprehensible, fashion, a much greater man than even Berkeley, viz. Descartes, the originator and founder of Modern Philosophy, as he is accurately described by Schwegler. (See Mill's *Logic*, 1843, vol. ii. p. 447.) *Primâ facie* it is simply incredible that even a tenth-rate speculator, (say, a vapid brassy leader of the *Revulsion*,) should have written the trash here imputed to Descartes ; and after due research I venture to assert that nothing like this summary can be found in any of the works of Descartes. As a fact, there is nothing of the sort (where, if anywhere, it should be) either in the Fourth Part of the *Discours*, or in the Fifth *Meditation*. It is an awakening piece of evidence, attesting the poverty-stricken state of English intelligence, that this work of Mr. Mill's, which teems with material mistakes and perversions, such as are contained in no other work of the kind, should have ever been received as a standard treatise on Logic. It is, however, constructed with considerable art, and written with an imposing breadth of style. These are excellent qualities in themselves ; but what if they only serve to cover poverty of thought and random assertion ?

stated as Kant states it. Space differs from odour, colour, &c., as being a form of *general sense*, and so valid for all sentient beings. As such, it is a subjective condition of mind in one of its kinds, viz. *Anschauung*, or figurate perception; usually rendered by the word *intuition*. Accordingly the phrase " as a condition of our minds," though not incorrect, lacks speciality, for it fits the Hamiltonian view of space, viz. that *a priori* space is a form of mental *activity* (discursive), *i.e.* a form or condition of thought as thought, as well as the Kantian view of space, viz. that it is a form of mental *receptivity* (intuitive), and not a form or condition of thought. Here, then, is an insufficiency in the expression of the question, which argues a looseness of apprehension in the Examiner.

But when it is said that Kant treats space as *not existing in the objects we behold*, he is mis-stating Kant's doctrines altogether. The empirical existence of what we behold is involved in the transcendental ideality of space; and space is, in that regard, an empirical condition of phenomena, and so does empirically exist in the objects we behold. If Kant denied this, which he does not, he would indeed be making all phenomena illusory. An Examiner who had an accurate knowledge of Kant's Æsthetic, simply *could not* have committed himself to such a question. The student who should read it literally and answer it intelligently would lose marks. This would be his answer : *Kant does not answer the objection; for it is an objection to Berkeley, and Kant implicitly allows its validity.* The other question is as follows:—

" Explain Kant's saying that experience is the first product of the understanding. How does his method differ from that of previous psychologists? How would you distinguish the constituent elements of (philosophical) experience?"

Does Kant say so quite *trocken?* Whether or not the question is a good one, likely to broach any knowledge the student may have on the Kantian doctrine of *Synthesis before Analysis.* The two following inquiries follow naturally, and will serve. If the student knows the double *rôle* played by Imagination in Kant's system, he will assuredly set forth that knowledge on the hint of the last inquiry. However, the word " (philosophical) " seems introduced for no other purpose than to baffle the examinee. " Transcendental" is the right word there ; was the Examiner afraid of it?

The remaining three questions on Kant in the papers of 1868 in Mental Philosophy do not remove the impression occasioned by these two, that the Examiners were not *au fait* with this philosophical system. The most important of these is as follows :

" Geometry is a science which determines the properties of space synthetically, and yet *à priori.*" Illustrate this sentence from Sir W. Hamilton's statement of the method in [*i.e.* on] which all philosophical inquiries must be pursued."

Now here we have Kant's own words in the *Transcendental Æsthetic :* so far, then, I have nothing to object. But the doctrine thus correctly rendered cannot be properly illustrated from Sir W. Hamilton's doctrine of method : and for this simple reason, that Hamilton, so far as he understood Kant's doctrine, (and this was not far,) rejected it : in fact, he rejected it wholly and utterly, without being quite aware of it. Hamilton taught that all synthesis is based on analysis ; and that we always analyse before we synthesyse. His doctrine is thus summed up by himself, " Synthesis without a previous analysis is baseless." (*Lectures on Metaphysics*, vol. i. p. 98.) Kant, on the contrary, founded his metaphysical system for no other conceivable end than to prove that *a priori* (*transcendental*) synthesis of understanding necessarily precedes all (*empirical*) analysis; and that it is thus that we get " synthetical judgments *a priori.*" Here, then, is a yawning abyss between Kant and Hamilton, of which the Examiners do not seem to have been at all aware. However, despite this abyss, Kant and Hamilton (borrowing of Kant in all blindness) teach that Geometry is a science which starts with its own axiomatic conceptions and definitions, and works from those generals down to the particular and even the individual ; and that all philosophical investigations must be pursued *on the opposite method*, *i.e.* starting with particulars and working up to general conceptions and propositions (what Lord Bacon called *axioms*), and ending with definitions. To call the latter an illustration of the former is simply misleading. We usually illustrate like by like, not unlike by unlike.

If the question have another meaning which

has escaped my scrutiny, I can only say, it is very strangely worded, and no student would be likely to make his marks out of it, save by the special indulgence of the Examiner : an indulgence accorded rather to the author of the question than to the questionist. Another is as follows :—

" Why do Æsthetics occupy the first place in Kant's Critique of the Pure Reason ? What topics are included under that title ? What is his next division ?"

It is a fair question. The student ought most clearly to apprehend the synthetic form of Kant's work, which is developed in the order of nature, and not in that of experience, *i.e.* Æsthetic before Logic, Logic before Dialectic ; and also the transcendental before the empirical, and the immanent before the transcendent. The second question follows naturally, but is insignificant. The third is trifling, unless it is intended to elicit a comparison between *Theil* and *Abtheilung ;* for the *next* Part is the *other* Part ; and the next *Division* is but itself a part of a Part.

And lastly we have this, which is a transparent catch-question :—

" What do Kant and Hamilton affirm as to the possibility of our knowing any things as they are in themselves ?"

It is, at any rate, on all accounts, very *safely* worded.

With these five questions in Mental Philosophy, having reference to the *Critic of Pure Reason,* may be compared the following five questions on the same work, which occur in a paper set by Mr. Mahaffy, Tutor of Trinity College, Dublin, in the Moderatorship Examination, of last Michaelmas Term, in that University. I suppose it is owing to the Examiners being, for the most part, Irishmen, that these questions occur in a paper on Ethics, and that it is customary in the University of Dublin to attach the note of interrogation to a mere assertion, as in the fifth question following :—

" 1. What does Kant mean by a schema? Into what error has Mr. Mansel fallen on this point?

2. How did Kant criticise Hume's doctrine of causality?

3. Explain Kant's use of the words *judgment, reflection* and *idea.*

4. Explain the statement that his doctrine of Space and Time is based on a *transcendental distinction.*

5. ' *Gigni de nihilo nihil, in nihilum nil posse reverti.*' This proposition is applied more cautiously by Kant than by Hamilton?"

The third is a sterile question, and the fourth, to say the least, very oddly worded. Whose statement? Not Kant's I think; nor yet Professor Kuno Fischer's, whose work on Kant was probably in the mind of the Examiner.

The last would have been more fruitful had it inquired on what grounds Hegel denounced the enunciated maxim as a truism. On the whole, these five questions do not show to great advantage beside the five set by the Cambridge Examiners. This is the more remarkable, as Dublin possesses some very good metaphysicians of the Kantian school, such as Mr. Mahaffy, Mr. Abbott, and Mr. Stanley-Monck.

In the Cambridge papers of 1869, in Moral Philosophy, appear five questions on Kant's Ethics. They are as follow :—

"Compare the doctrines of Butler and of Kant respecting Self-love.

"What is Kant's definition of a Free Will? How does he distinguish negative from positive Freedom?

"Explain the words Autonomy and Heteronomy according to Kant's use of them.

"How does Kant distinguish Legality from Morality? Do you remember any attempts to distinguish them in other writers? Kant says that 'a dog or a horse may be an object of *affection*, a wild beast or the sea of *dread*.' What does he affirm to be the only objects of *Reverence*?

"How did Kant propose to deal with the antitheses *perfection* and *happiness*, *self* and *others*? What philosophers had he chiefly in mind in this adjustment? What new point of view did he supply himself?"

The second and third relate to the same topic, and might be answered together in a breath : the enquiry nevertheless is proper, and the other questions, if less important, are well enough. I find no fault with these five questions : but I am surprised that they should not have been supplemented (or even superseded, if space and time were wanting,) by questions touching the principles of Kant's Ethical system. The defect I feel in this regard is not so noticeable in the questions on Plato and Aristotle, where one is used to the dry " inductive lights," and expects, as of course, the usual externalities of the schools.

In this one word, *externalities*, is summed up the manifold deficiencies of these Cambridge Examina-

G

tion-papers, as well in Mental as in Moral Philosophy. The questions are the mere *aperçus* of outsiders. An Examiner who had placed himself at the centre of a philosophical system could hardly help showing, by the ring or form of his questions, some evidence of his intellectual mastery and grasp. Few of the questions in these papers show anything of the kind ; and the best of them is nervous with the temerity or timidity of minds who are as empty of the central intelligence as they are as full of " the literature of the subject."

If, however, it is just this latter, and hardly at all the former, that they look for in the candidates, and which the Board looks for in the Examiners themselves, it is, then, for the Professor of Moral Philosophy to impose upon all three a higher view of their vocations. Philosophy, like any of its subordinate sciences, is necessarily rooted in the past, and has its history and its literature, which no student can with impunity neglect. But, like them, Philosophy is the subject of an *a priori* organon, and the one business of the philosopher is to render it perfect. The student, who is to become a philosopher, should not be taught to " walk ever with reverted eyes."

ERRATA.

Page 59, *prefix to* l. 26 *the word* of.
,,   79   ,,   ,, ,, 14 ,, ,,   Analytical.
,,   82   ,,   8, *for* is *read* are.

tion-papers, as well in Mental as in Moral Philosophy.
The questions are the mere *aperçus* of outsiders. An
Examiner who had placed himself at the centre of a
philosophical system could hardly help showing, by
the ring or form of his questions, some evidence of
his intellectual mastery and grasp. Few of the questions in these papers show anything of the kind ; and
the best of them is nervous with the temerity or
· ·¹⁴~ ₒf minds who are as empty of the central
‾ ‾ ·· ₑ " ⁴ₕₒ literature of

themselves, iₗ iₛ, ₜₕₑₙ,
Philosophy to impose upon all three a higher ᵥᵢₑ~
of their vocations. Philosophy, like any of its
subordinate sciences, is necessarily rooted in the
past, and has its history and its literature, which no
student can with impunity neglect. But, like them,
Philosophy is the subject of an *a priori* organon, and
the one business of the philosopher is to render it
perfect. The student, who is to become a philosopher, should not be taught to " walk ever with
reverted eyes."

www.ingramcontent.com/pod-product-compliance
Lightning Source LLC
Chambersburg PA
CBHW020315090426

42735CB00009B/1351